EZEKIEL'S WHEELS

BOOKS BY SHIRLEY KAUFMAN

POETRY

Ezekiel's Wheels
Threshold
Roots in the Air: New & Selected Poems
Rivers of Salt
Claims
From One Life to Another
*Looking at Henry Moore's Elephant Skull Etchings in Jerusalem During
    the War*
Gold Country
The Floor Keeps Turning

TRANSLATIONS

The Flower of Anarchy: Selected Poems of Meir Wieseltier
But What: Selected Poems of Judith Herzberg (with the poet)
My Little Sister and Selected Poems, poems by Abba Kovner
The Light of Lost Suns, poems by Amir Gilboa
A Canopy in the Desert, poems by Abba Kovner

ANTHOLOGY

The Defiant Muse: Hebrew Feminist Poems from Antiquity to the Present
    (co-edited with Galit Hasan-Rokem and Tamar S. Hess)

Ezekiel's Wheels

SHIRLEY KAUFMAN

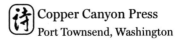 Copper Canyon Press
Port Townsend, Washington

Cover art: Odilon Redon (1840–1916), *The Eye like a Strange Balloon Mounts toward Infinity*, 1882. Charcoal on paper, 16.625 × 13.125 inches. Gift of Larry Aldrich. The Museum of Modern Art, New York. Digital image copyright the Museum of Modern Art / Licensed by SCALA / Art Resource, New York.

Our gratitude to the editors of the following publications, where some of these poems, often in earlier versions, first appeared:

> *American Poetry Review, Bridges, European Judaism, Field, Hunger Mountain Review, Maggid, Narrative Inc., Poetry East, Runes, Water-Stone Review, Zeek*

> *Poets Against the War*, edited by Sam Hamill, Thunder's Mouth Press / Nation Books, 2003.

Copper Canyon Press is in residence at Fort Worden State Park in Port Townsend, Washington, under the auspices of Centrum. Centrum is a gathering place for artists and creative thinkers from around the world, students of all ages and backgrounds, and audiences seeking extraordinary cultural enrichment.

LIBRARY OF CONGRESS CATALOGING-IN-PUBLICATION DATA

Kaufman, Shirley.
Ezekiel's wheels / Shirley Kaufman.
  p. cm.
ISBN 978-1-55659-307-9 (pbk.: alk. paper)
1. Jews — Poetry.   I. Title.
PS3561.A862E94 2009
811′.54 — dc22

                                    2009024443

9 8 7 6 5 4 3 2 FIRST PRINTING

COPPER CANYON PRESS
Post Office Box 271
Port Townsend, Washington 98368

www.coppercanyonpress.org

Always for Bill
and for our families

Contents

EZEKIEL'S WHEELS

Prologue: Where Am I?

I'm not sure
I don't know where
I'm going anymore
heading into the footlights
I had meant to say "front lights"
no I had not meant cars
but spots I mean
spotlights the kind you step into
on a stage well maybe it really was
footlights the beams that focus
only on you for the time you are
speaking your lines
but if you forget them
without a prompter
the lights on the words
will forget you or leave you alone
in the dark in the absence
of what you've forgotten.

So where was I
no the question is always
where am I
only I think if I say it
in the past
it will stay in the past
or somewhere I can forget it.

The first rule I learned
in Hebrew was that the verb
to be has no present.

3

Nothing that simply *is*
though it feels familiar.
We're only a pause
on a spiraling run.

I want to step forward
into the impossible
but I'm afraid if I look
at life too steady and too hard
it will burn straight through me.

Your Place

You wait at the side
like an opera extra
told where to be
when the curtain rises.
Position is everything
when you have nothing
to say and nowhere
to move. And even if
it doesn't matter whether
you're told to stand or sit
it seems quite crucial
to know your place.

.

The way you know
when to enter and leave
or who to take notice of
and who not. And why
you must learn the rules
of engagement as if
you line up
for battle every day.

Why do we think
our encounters
will turn out dangerous?
Why do we have to
prepare ourselves
to survive? As if birth
itself were not

something we managed
bloody and screaming
but alive.

The Test

You place the palm of your hand
beneath each breast
and lift them one at a time
onto a glass shelf
as the weight of another shelf
comes down and presses them hard.
Between the punishing surface
of each layer of glass
your squeezable flesh.
Both arms stretch out,
your hands clasp the shining bars
for respite but there is none.

And if you decide between
testing yourself the old ways
or jumping dizzy into
a whirlpool of finders keepers
losers weepers
not daring to know
what the end might be,
when you rise up for air
you will be blinded by light.

So you come to the place
where the road ends
and there's nothing ahead.
You can stand on the edge
and tremble with fear
or risk your life and jump
to the other side.

What Matters

We're into it. The new year
already frayed and worn out
at the edges and even February
ready to sneak away. I was never
able to make anything stand still.
And now the days slip past as if
they want to leave me behind.

I don't want to stay behind
with the slow ones who are
never sure where they are
going or whether they want
to move. Not that I'm sure,
but I want to be able to act
when something is urgent.

Like saving a life or stopping
the next war. As crucial
as that. What's the point of
exerting oneself if it isn't
crucial. If it won't make any
difference to whether you
live or die. That sort of magic.

I always wanted to do what
matters. To stand at the center
of the stage and deliver my lines
so that people choke with tears
or fall down laughing. So that

we all wake up the next morning
and change ourselves

maybe even the world.

Hope

Through a blue window
I am letting it go, light
having washed its feathers.

The sky is a flat sheet
of water reflecting itself,
and when I face

its immeasurable underside,
there's nothing behind it.
Only a darkening space

for me to curl under. Snug
in the spell of a cradle
rocking, I remember

the first time I floated
on my back as a child,
the unflappable calm,

as if I were slipping into
the future where the light
was waiting to come back,

and where I would find
my lost breath again
after I drowned.

Safe

As in better to be safe
than sorry. Everything unknown
safely within bounds.
The world turning as it always does
toward light in the morning,
nothing to do with the breakfast news.

Not the flight of a dove, the longed-for,
nor the risk of the artist
who faces the bird with arms extended
almost like wings.

Nor this one-eyed wife
who flies without instruments
in a chancy climate,
still dazzled by words.

She keeps wanting it both ways,
little tooth marks all over her heart.

Return from the Dead Sea

isn't a return to life
or an escape from death.
The sea keeps shrinking.

We're warned not to
risk our lives on that floor
where the sinkholes are waiting:

another danger, as if each
waking moment and even sleep
weren't scary enough.

The sky drops lower like the sea,
they meet at an ink blue line
where the world ends.

There were days when
they sheltered each other
as we breathed through each other's lips.

Now the space between sea
and memory grows wider.
We're part of the distance.

Listen

Not to the woodpecker drilling
the wormy bark of our jacaranda,
not to the smothered words in our throats
as we lose and forget,
not even to our secret prayers.

What would happen if all I heard
were the lapping of leaves at our window,
the lift of your eyelids waking,

the sound in my ear of an echoing shell
with its infinite waters,
of a voice that has whispered ten thousand years
from a tiny slit in its face?

What if all I could hear were chants of creation,
clear thunder of chaos, original wonder and fear —

if all we listened to
was under us like seeds
and the purposeful wriggling of worms?

Circle

for Aliza Auerbach

1. PASSAGE

A sudden dazzle from above
as if a third eye, great disk of light
shines through the widened hole

and stuns the new child.
How does it get to the outside,
pushed from the sheltering cave,

muck and chaos of the dark canal,
ripped flesh left by its head
emerging? It enters history in blindness

not ready to see what the world is.
Memory begins its fine tracing in the brain
so even the frenzied thrust is recorded,

the panic already learned. Perhaps
the way out is always like this:
pressed through one's blindness

into the terrible dawn of light.

2. FIRST LIFE

If you begin with terror, primal
cry of the newborn, eyes first blinking
from the womb-world into the unknown light,

if you begin with the cut that splits it
forever from its first home, blood slimy
on the face, the clutching fingers,
if you begin with a body's weight
first measured in the lifting arms,
a human touch to lessen the fright,

life becomes what it is and is not only
a slippery cord severed at both ends.

3. LAST LIFE

The wrinkles on your mother's face track
her passage back to beginnings.
Creases run down the sides

of mountains when the ice thaws.
Nothing can stop them.
She is becoming a mountain.

Her separate selves are one now.
She bears them willingly like weather:
wind and salt spray, weathered love.

Her life is a circle in which she skates
down the hills with the children,
or swims in the sea every day

out and back to the crumbling shore.
The skin of the earth cracks
from the strain of holding itself together.

She keeps her wholeness.
Her wrinkles have a woman in them
brushing the light. It shines

where the luminous waves are braided
and fastened to the top of her head
with a comb. It shines on her hair.

Succot

I raise my eyes to heaven
but the three balconies get in my way,
no more than the code allows
on our street in Jerusalem,
and most of them with frail booths
for this week when families
bless what they can
and share their food.

My bearded grandfather sat alone
in his sanctum next to the kitchen door
where his last two unmarried
daughters brought him his food.
He looked like a prince in his
tailored suit and shiny skullcap,
waited on by my aunts who were
careful not to spill the soup.

He made his own wine from
the cherry tree that blazed
in his garden, first sign of spring.
My cousin used to climb there
when the fruit was ripe
and shake the red cherries loose
and squashable over me. He shook,
I ran and caught what I could.

Some mornings I wake
when my room is still dark
and my eyes don't focus.

17

I seem to see more when I cannot
see. Like the sparks of
what circles around me
when I remember the child
I thought I was.

In the Recovery Room

1. BREASTSTROKE

Grandpa swims out with me
in his striped one-piece
thirties bathing suit
                        both of us
ease our palms together
in cautious prayer

before our hands sweep
backward
                under the surface

his white beard
                        flows
with the water

we kick like frogs
                        and soft
as a girl's
                his white arms

pull me
                to shore

2. YOU

Your face trembles
out of a cloud
        the light
around it like a wreath of
nasturtiums I sucked the honey from
when I was a child
everything's white and orange
on the stage at Epidaurus
we're playing against the gods
in white togas

your lips swim into focus
                smiling
I can't hear the good news

you brush my mouth
too lightly as if you're afraid
to touch me

        suddenly
one of us is gone

3. FLIGHT

After takeoff I look back
at the shoreline
waves unroll their shrouds
layer by layer over the edge

after the shoreline
sunlit icecaps drift

without will or direction
away from the graves

after the icecaps
strapped in my capsule
there's nothing to see
but a vagueness of clouds

after I left you
stood there watching
as if you were also waiting
for somewhere to land

4. LEMON TREE

From the sidewalk Sam waves
over the plumbagos
little mercies of blue
where I'm weeding the garden
I straighten my back
and he gives me advice
about our ailing lemon

two people scream
on the other side of the room
a nurse
              hovers between them
with needles

                  and I can't hear
what to do with the lemon
or even the buzzing of summer

only the groundwater
rising
           over my body
where I cannot move

5. ABSENCE

My soul's on the ceiling
and it won't come down

6. UNCERTAINTIES

When you've been given
a second chance
                you need
to care more (less)
about what you live for

not so much staying alive

as the old skin you wear
the everyday sloughing

Mother

swamps in the soup pot
oatmeal erupting all over
the stove
    who took my
tweezers there's a bead
in her ear
    we have to
give thanks for
scorched lamb chops?

guinea pigs coming
and coming
why isn't Gigi back
in the cage
we're all out of sawdust

her children
leave

    she cleans out
the turds
    she's wasted
her words

what did she mean
when she didn't...

2

if there were no way
for a mother
to remember the good times
she would roll herself
in her blankets
and never come out

what goes on
in her romantic mind
that tangles her thoughts
and willing connections
what hides in the clutter
she can't see through

when the children have gone
through the door
she left open

will she know
who she is

who she has to forgive?

Care

If I spoke to you now
something I'd say
formed out of words
you could recognize

what would you hear?
Saying and hearing
live in two separate
worlds and we can't

always bring them
together. I don't know
what you're hearing
when I say a word

that means something
special to me. What
does it mean to you?
Care, for instance.

Instance, for instance.
Waves of meaning
lap over each other
and leave only froth

on the shore. Okay
to wade in or sit
on a beach chair
there with your toes

in the water, diddling
the surf. White foam
lathers my toes. Do
you care for my toes?

For instance.

Art

Turner had himself tied
to the mast of a ship
to experience a storm at sea.

Every sailor was ordered
below deck
                   only the painter
and the waves.

                   Only
the risk of surrender
the first time we love.

How tight we hang on
to keep from drowning.

Bench

after a photograph by Garry Winogrand

Their shoes are flat and sturdy
meant for a day of walking
even taking a pause
in the unposed photograph
that cancels their breath.

Growing up I was taught
not to push. Why do they
all sit so closely together?
Not enough benches?

The man on the end is only
half there, half of him
reading half of the news.

If I were sitting by myself
on a bench in the park
I'd be looking at nothing
not looking at grass or a path
but absence.

       The world is
too much not with me. I'm
only two eyes with no head
watching no presence no
writing in the sky.

I wish I could fly I wish
I could drift through the park
like a leaf
      the softness of air
on my skin the stir of new
words in my mouth.

Nothing

Nothing between me and the clouds
or me and the earth. Butch Hancock
said he learned to tune his tractor
to the key of G when he was a kid,
wrote his songs plowing the fields
in Lubbock.
            I'm trying to think
how high I would have to be
standing on the highest hill
how low
            lying on my back
in a plowed field before
it is planted. I want to stretch
my arms until I feel my fingers
touching the space that's nothing.
To press the skin of my back
so hard against the ground
that I can feel the absence below.

We're born feeling something.
Tiny sensors in our throats start
the first cry. We don't have to
ask why. There's nothing
between our wanting
and our need. It begins
in the seed. And the sprouting.
The hunger we're driven to feed.
So why does nothing stand
in the way
            with its lumpy presence?

Ezekiel's Wheels

1

Getting used to it
used to what
what
            Going blind. What?
what what
                        Circles too big
for one eye

Half a whirl at a time
take the frying pan
off take the lid off
close the lid-under-the-lid
to stop the wheels

Likeness of firmament
color of the terrible ice

Circles
            without any end
catch fire catch flame catch
what

            so fierce I'll never catch
hold

            Hellfires

But *the heavens were opened*
Ezekiel's chariot and its wheels
wheel within wheel

mad dog chasing its tail
heavenhound hellhound

Circles
              without any

        2

Used to it Wheels
and their turnings

The glory came down
but I must have
missed it

              cloud with a fire
flashing up
                      and out of the fire
came lightning came
coals burning like torches

and rainbows circling my lamp
the globe in my ceiling the

brightness around it

seen through the cloud
that covers my eye

32

3

And my room was filled
with clouds
            and the window

full of the brightness

and the wheel was full of eyes
that spin in every
direction

            as good as a
poem (a life)
                        what comes from
the eye
            takes in gives out

till the muddle begins
the muck I sink into

churning my way in my bed
to the Library for the Visually
Impaired

            imperiled
impaled
on shutters that have closed

4

"Offer a path to which we can
say yes," he writes

                      but not
in blindness and fury...

My friend who draws birds
in their flight
                 who lives in the

brightness around it
without any cloud

Intuitive eye of the artist
pencil and brush
and catchable wings

the noise of their wings
like the noise of great waters

5

The heavens were opened
but not to me

               never

to unbelievers pinched
in the crack between faith
and reluctance

What can
my eyes wake up to what
vision of Ezekiel in exile
or holiness ever

Where
will I find him

in the midst of the valley
and it was full of bones

6

Ezekiel cried, Dem dry bones!
Ezekiel cried, Dem dry bones!
Ezekiel cried, Dem dry bones!
Oh hear the word of the Lord.

Dem bones, dem bones gon-na
walk a-roun'
Dem bones, dem bones gon-na

fix those eyes those bones those bones
gonna fix those eyes oh hear
the word of these eyes

7

If the eye can sing
before it sees
if the tongue
can find words before it

why sit
in an unfinished waiting room
waiting for something to happen

The pressure goes up and the veil
comes

      down

where the song is
down in the black swamp

as if only white pills

in the midst of the valley
full of dry bones

He named it depression

   8

"One must admire black," said
Redon

     out of his terrors
discovering the not-seen
hiding in corners
          or inside
somebody else's nightmare

his eyeball travels up
in a basket

the half-seen
something beyond sad faces
of childhood beyond the visible
giant eyeball

Redon named it
The Eye like a Strange Balloon
Mounts toward Infinity

the monster eye won't
leave me alone
                    caught in a stare
of nothing more perfect

9

Blindness
              seeps into
variables of light
changed by the hour

Monet's pond with water lilies
clusters of
              water lilies
in Giverny the flowers themselves
like splashes calmed down

more delicate
                    fragile as halos
festoons pale garlands

and Monet's vision
diminished as if through
the haze of a dream
                    wheels
twirling and turning
is that what I saw or he

speed
disintegrating

                Monet
Monet
        his damaged sight

huge sweep of his brush
and the shimmer of water lilies
like memories of light

        10

And poor old Homer blind
blind as a bat

                    repeating it twice
with Eleanor/Helen
                    man-
destroying city-destroying
what-else-
            destroying
blind as a bat
how blind is that

11

How blind is anyone

turning away
                    refusing
to see how blind
are the locked-out

who can't see
how the doors close

just when a small crack
of light is
                    full of the brightness

12

O dark dark...
                    amid the blaze

Eyeless in Gaza

                    What kind of
woman
            Helen Delilah
their craft and dazzle

squeeze the power
like a wet rag

what's left what's
limp

Betrayed he
shook the two pillars
till it all collapsed

Ashes ashes
                    they all fall down

          13

The poet heard it
in the blazing center

of his lost Paradise

heard the words
he could not see
quickening the thick flames

the whirlwind sound of
wheel within wheel
                    fire
in the spokes

          14

               And fear
the gradual fear of it

Would it be easy
all at once
               or stuttering
not yet

                little by little
         what's little
                        what what
         Small bites
                        morsels of horror

         15

         Waiting
         for something to save me

         If you open your mind to
         irrelevant traps
                          to what will you
         open your eyes

                         My life
         in its blur and its panic

         anyone else's is safer
         quotations are safer

         not able
         to give up this
         blindness
                        I've said it

         this light that's enough
         as if there were ever

         true seeing

16

Do I know when I see
you I'm not seeing

who you are or

who I am in the mirror
looking at myself

or who you are
eating breakfast
not knowing who we are

not seeing not hearing
not able
            not notable
after so many years

two wheels locked
in their tracks still
turning still
            getting derailed

till death do thee part

or we find our way
out of Knossos
following Ariadne's thread

17

Nobody's story but my own
coming to an end

                          Could this
be coming to

yes no
            not wanting
not ever forever

used to it
            never
coming to an end

Blindness deepens
its blindness

plugs a hole in the curtain
plugs another hole

then waits for the next

18

When Borges took charge
of the Library with half
of one eye
            he could
recognize the bindings

He read in memory
what he could not see

I live among vague luminous
shapes that are not darkness yet

    not fear and frenzy
    not absent horizons

but fingers held up to
my eyes
      wait
widen the spaces between them

four sentinels of the prophet

flesh/bone
edging out of the dark
trembling to be seen

I'm not ready for shapes yet
or gasping descriptions

wanting the unseen more than

not ready to give it up

   19

Wanting too much can you
ever

Ezekiel in his exile
captive in a foreign land

longing

until *the heavens were opened*

The sky's blue lid still
closes on fire
          and Ezekiel's wheel
climbs to the top of the sky now

in heavenly flame

          I'd roll
to the bottom of the hill I fell on
as a child
          longing to fly

roll and roll over
flattening the spring grass
unsettling the air

          inhaling
the green on my skin
green spring in my breath

beginning

          my longing
without end

20

in memory of Ruth Levin

Sitting next to my old friend
dying
      her skittery mind

"What will become of them?"
she whispers
         as if they were
small still
      rolling down hills
and she a young mother

Already late light darkens
her hennaed hair

she might be gone
         before morning
flickers
      across her bedroom wall

Her face will stay in my mind
the way it always
        when she
stands at her easel squinting
her eyes
      tilting her head unseen
to find where the brush goes

I'll see her fingers
on the handle

                    the way she dips
her brush into the paint
twists it to wipe the excess

before she lifts it up
to the unseen canvas

        21

I'm never sure if the day
is ending
                or the world

or whether the unseen
has replaced
what I used to see

Wheels and their turnings

can the mind provide
what the eye will
                        never

I remember thine eyes well
said the blind king

Limits

There's an end
always coming
toward us

like a hole
getting deeper
the farther you dig

or a poem
that eats up
its words.

If a poem had no limits
and simply went on
after it started

from one line
to another spilling
down a staircase

with no end,
it would still
run out of words

or stop when
the bottom arrived.
So here I am

knocked out
on the floor
where I get to

most of the time.
The only way I learn
how far I can go.

Stuck

Tomorrow a new walk is
a new walk, wrote Ammons.
Make it new, said Pound.

But a new walk is an old walk
after I stumble after I can't see
the cracks in the pavement.

I put one foot ahead of the other
unsure of my balance confused
about where I am going.

Once the machinery is stuck
someone might get it started
again but I'm an old model.

There are no new parts.

A Season of Birds

for Anthony Dubovsky

They come fluttering out of
my printer
            only one
with its wings spread
but I know they are flying.
How else would they get here?

Absolute attentiveness
for its own sake
Every flicker of the brush
like my reaching
for the right word.

And *love*. He wanted
to say that word as well

Chavela Vargas late in life
her smoky voice: *Pintor*
si pintas, con amor...

to be banned from Paradise
forever because of their
innocence
            not lust
not even greed
that longing in the mouth
only to taste

how it continues
in my bodiless mind
and somewhere between
the wings of my shoulders
even now especially
now

Epithalamium

for Sarah and Avrami

Your heads pop straight up through the hupa
like two corks of champagne,
taking the silkiness with you.

You must be dazzled
as you whiz to the edge of the blue
where it meets the Pacific,
and over the edge when the sun drops
and there are no limits,
no difference between lights on the shore
and stars
or what you find wordless in each other.

Look down, look down at the way
we all stand with our wishes and longings.
What about your dogs?

Something More

I lost the line it might have been
musically perceptive at least it was
singing in my head when suddenly
I was lifted out of the line
or the line blew away from me.
How far can I search
without stumbling over the edge
and into the old mess rotting below?
How deep can I reach into my mind
for significant thoughts like what
are we doing here what do we want
from the sea if we find it between
the umbrellas?

               I've had enough sky
enough sea I'm not even sure what
I wanted or what special words
curling out of the surf
over the white foam
with answers I need to know.

The Art of Submission

What could have made it less
difficult to think of giving up
this gray turning blue old world
outside. Tumor cut out
and the danger gone. Tick-tock.
Nothing blocked. What's left?
What can time care for if time
doesn't stop? Just see how it runs.
One blind mouse. Uphill.
Down. Runs out of breath.
Where does it go.
I'm the last one to know.

—

Softer than custard
that quivers on my plate.
*They also serve who only stand
and wait.* I live in a state of
held breath as if it's too hard
to believe I could ever be safe.
Submit or surrender.
What does that mean?
Not to dig my way out
if there is a way out. Is out
any different from in
with a muddle of doubt.

—

What has the art of submission
got to do with art? A gift
or a curse. Succor or
suffer. Anyone's choice.
Like choosing to play
your life in a minor key.
And call it music.
Should I believe the danger
is over. How much can I know.
The way I keep putting
one foot in front of the other
with no place to go.

Whole

Nothing will be whole again, she says
with a sigh too big for the room.
Whole as in certain. Whole as in
what we depend on.

            Not only ourselves.
Not the fenced world we took our first steps in
or the four tiny stents in the branches
of my heart.

           We move to the porch
where marigolds praise us over the sides
of their clay pots. Buds peel outward
like slippery tongues. Roses named Peace
are pink-rimmed and tagged
like newborns in hospital cribs.

We put little green rafts of mint
in our cups but they capsize.
The tea is fragrant. A drowned leaf
silky in my mouth. I swallow it whole.

Penelope

She woke every morning
surprised by light. Early
or not so early it came
through the slats of the blinds
like the blade of a skate.

Life was rushing ahead too fast
and she couldn't catch up
always having to hang on
to what she had
while stretching one arm ahead.
Whatever was out there
beyond her reach
she had to take hold of
but it stayed just beyond
her fingers and wouldn't be
caught.

        She didn't want to stay
home to stay where she was
surrounded by picture postcards
instead of the real thing.
She wanted to travel
not to sit in the same chair
at her computer
weaving words every night
she'd unravel by day.

Staglieno Cemetery in Genoa

I carry a twig from the avenue of trees
wanting to name the tree
if someone can tell me.
                    I touch the flowers
in all the bronze vases attached to the tombs
rubbing the petals between my fingers
to know if they're real. Chrysanthemums.
Especially roses. And tiny white puffs
of baby's breath. Such diligent imitation.
As if even life were not real.

I step between beds of marble.
Baby Malena Rossi smiling forever at age five.
Though the wings are too grand
for the sparrow flying over her name.

But the angels! Their loving arms.
Even the one who abandons herself
to inconsolable loss on the lid of a grave
white luster with weeping hair.
How much they care.
White luster.
                  Weeping hair.

Passages

for Aliza Auerbach

We enter these frames too late
to start over: fish, slender
as slits of the crocodile's eyes,
are trapped in their helpless panic.
White maggots feast in the belly
of a deer, flames freeze
the instant they flare, two roads
disappear.

       Huge blowups
of time between now and next.
No magic to ease the overwrought
minnows or haystacked trees
that want to be women.

Stunned in my own time warp,
losing my balance
while the words I might have said
still levitate in midair,
what were we on our way to
after here?
       What happens there?

After the Shine

We will become godlike
said the poet
because she was shining

but after the shine?
When the days become
links in a tarnished necklace
that used to be silver.

Don't talk about *after*
while the years fizzle out
like comets that once burned
tracks in the sky

tracks that blazed
over the rim of the world
where we were afraid to follow.

Why should we be afraid
after squeezing into our lives
through a hole we opened
with our own heads?

Losing My Mind

The thing about losing my mind,
which I am, in the middle of my
eighties, is that I can still act as if
I'm in control, and I am in control,
sort of, I just don't know where
anything is. I hope if I give this
a title, I'll know where to find it
when I want to see it again.
But if I forget the title, then what?

Of course, I'm not really scared
about losing my mind. It's right
where it always was, inside
my brain, covered up by my head.
But how can I count on its still
being there since there's nothing
to see and I'm not a believer?
Minds live in their own worlds,
and don't always let us in.

Maybe I'll have to coax it
to come out, the way I get down
on my knees next to the sofa
and say very gently: Kitty, kitty,
it's time to come out. Of course,
I offer her a saucer of milk
at the same time, something
to be seen or smelled. What
can I offer to my mind?

Advantages

there are advantages in abandoning punctuation
when it comes to cadence and organizing principles

and the integrity of the line the integrity of
anything that moves in a given direction

still managing to stay straight that begins
and ends without needing to make sense

nothing makes sense if you shine a light
on it for a long time not even so long

Too Late

Each year more alien more peripheral
over your doorsill with my shoes off
what can I say near midnight
when your children are read to and asleep
and you roll out two pie crusts for apples
starting to ferment.
                              It's always too late
pears rot wherever they drop and staked
in the garden tomatoes already too soft.

Too late or too many (you'd never say) prayers
kids screeching and pots in the sink
eight fugitive chickens someone
has asked you to keep for too long.
They scratch in the dry grass run around
clucking and lay a few eggs.

Dear woman dear daughter dear
life I am no longer part of
dear inescapable presence
it's always too many too late
for the garden too late for the pies
and my helpless hugging too much
too hurting too (not enough) loving.

Letting It Out

I don't want you to stand
with your smile on and stare
at the lip of my wound.
The infection starts deeper.

I need to live like an orange
in its sweet flesh, peel the rind
of my own skin the way you do
in one unbroken spiral.

I feel that the future's behind us.
We'll have to grow eyes
in the back of our heads
to know where we're going.

You've finished your
paint-by-number picture
of the river Lethe. I can't
stay inside the lines.

I hide poems under my pillow
I don't want you to tell me
to look for grammatical errors
and what about dinner.

Locked In

If I could tell you what I need most
to say but never gets said
because the words won't come into
my head, my mouth can't put them
into sounds that you would hear,
not that I whisper, it's just that
they can't get out of the space
they're locked in, closed to anyone
who doesn't know how to listen.

They're locked forever inside me
because you don't know the password
or knew it and then forgot it
and I've forgotten it too. We're losing
our trust. How did we get to this
impossible impasse how can we
get out of it? If we tell each other
the stories of our lives will we finish
in time?

Lost

The sky is empty most of the time.
What we can't pray to isn't there.
What happened yesterday is lost
and will be lost tomorrow.
Forgetting repeats itself
like smoldering ashes
still heating the hearth
or shards in the wadis
after the streams have dried.
Sometimes a flicker of quartz
or mica among the stones.

The earth is warming
and nothing sprouts
in the reluctant sand.

What if the world burns up
and we don't burn with it?
Here in the wilderness of Sinai
will anyone find us and take us in?

It's not

a real emptiness
the sense of nothing
but a sinkhole
sucking me in.

           I was waiting
for life to happen
the way I always
check the days on my calendar
make my lists.

           I don't want to
look back but can't see ahead
from where I am now

and *now* is whatever I didn't do
yesterday. Not what I live in.
Now is the fear
there won't be anything
after now.

Avian Influenza, 2004

Is it the curve of their beaks
is it the pitiful squeaks

is it the fatal illness
is it their squawking panic

should they stop laying eggs
and hide in the henhouse

should they be less than human
when humans kill them

dumping them into pits
tossing them into trenches

living bodies trembling
hysterical flapping of

Cyclamen

And when it was claimed
the war had ended, it had not ended.
DENISE LEVERTOV, "IN CALIFORNIA
DURING THE GULF WAR"

They are fragile, pale apparitions
among the stones after the heavy rains,
as if to tell us, "We're back,
you have to take notice."

Rosy and white like spun-sugar wings
about to take off,
their tremblings alert us again
to possibility.

No more than that. While the planes
roar and practice over our heads,
and we dutifully buy bottled water,
tape for our sealed rooms,

and check our gas masks.
Caught in the same efficiency
that kills. How many rallies
singing songs of peace?
How many wars?

January 29, 2003
Jerusalem

Kite Festival at the Israel Museum

Kites

over Noguchi's sculpture garden
flying north

    fathers are letting out
    the lines

a festival of forgetting
in the middle of a war

    their kids ride in tanks
    no strings to hang on to

Under

for O.E.

Eight years on the base
the pilots the wives the kids

she was pregnant again
when he went up the last time

somebody saw his plane hit
watched the swing of his body

parachute open and drifting
under the sea's white froth

tangle of rope and nylon
rise and fall of the water

the sea smoothing its feathers

Piece by piece

it's crumbling
falling apart
and the pieces get lost
I'm not even sure
what they are

some leftover scraps
of memory

old scraps
to fasten my life down
like tent pins
to keep it
from blowing away.

When I was young
new thoughts were
sizzling in my brain
as if about to catch fire.
Maybe they did.
Maybe they burnt
themselves out before
I was ready.

How ready is ready?
What do I know about
being prepared when
I still don't know
what to prepare for.

The Governor of Somewhere

for Anthony Dubovsky

The governor of somewhere
shot a moose: he called it
"a badge of distinction" but added
"not for the moose."

Then he announced that suffrage
is still incomplete. He proposed
getting on with it: give the vote
now to insects, katydids, fireflies.

"Mind the bushes," he said,
and "furnish the fields." Food
for all, leaf by leaf — from each
according to ability, to each

according to his need.
Then followed the last and quite
cryptic line: "Oh yes, and keep
the darkness dark as well..."

I'm leaving three dots at the end
as a sign that something's
unfinished, or perhaps to extend
the mystery. What else can I do

when he drifted off
at the end, leaving me
alone at the edge,
too scared to look over.

U-turn

She sits on the shady side
because it's hot and she's tired
of running away. No clouds
in the canopy over the valley
the silky distance above
the trees and the buildings
beyond.
          No sound until
a bus pulls in across the street.

She closes and opens her eyes
as a man walks by dangling
two plastic bags he must have
brought home from the market.

She hasn't shopped for their
dinner. She doesn't want to
go home. A car makes a U-turn
in front of her bench as if
it were going the wrong way.
Which way is right?
Now a taxi is also turning around.

If they can't be wherever
they came from
where else will they go?

Only Child

She stood at my door
in the dream and I could
hear her extravagant voice: You
only you no one but you
and then I'm finished
any more I'll get rid of.

So when they told me later
she had lost the last one
I figured out what she'd done.
She didn't want anyone but me
no other daughter or son no
sister no brother.

I saw the small body quiver
and try to swim or grab on
to the sides of the toilet
with tiny fat fingers
but after the gush
of water
        it was gone.

Metamorphosis

> Death is the shape of being that is left behind.
> OVID

The shape we give it
tight lips of unbearable pain
laments of loss

or merciful laughter
our prints in the sand
the sea washed over

we never see the little
dead cells
we wipe from our skin

our minds won't know
who we wanted to be
or even who we became.

Unwinding

September is running out of days. Each night
the light slips over and under a little sooner,
each day the crisp leaves loosen their grip
and drift downward in slow motion
just as we used to play reels back again
to admire the diver's grace unwinding.

But I am frightened of unwinding,
divers who disappear. Night after night
on a painted horse I'm dizzy again
going up and down. The music stops sooner
than I expected. Along with the motion.
My hands circle its neck, unsure of my grip,

as if I were clutching at memory's grip,
confused by my mind's unwinding:
the music, the carousel, motion
of all my carelessness, days and nights —
how I want to retrieve them sooner
not later, and never let them go again.

What is it that scares me? What is it again
in my slippery mind that cannot grip
and hang on? Or slips from under me sooner
than I am ready, my life unwinding
scrolls of unwritten words. Some nights
I feel like a diver, afraid of motion,

whose grace is lost. And then the motion,
the graceless motion, begins again
and again through theatrical nights
of bad dreams. I'm bruised by the grip
of my struggle with winding, unwinding.
I wish I could heal it sooner

than leaves lose fire. But what we want sooner
comes less and less when we try. Motion
goes nowhere, each gesture of sweet unwinding
is just a gesture of sadness. Again and again
we try it, wanting to feel what we used to. The grip
of knowing ourselves in each other every night.

Every day is like night, when sooner
than I can find my grip, the motion
goes nowhere again, winding, unwinding.

Parables for Aging

1

Give up
what you look for.
Open the window
so the wind can blow
your desk clean.

2

Go home
when you're tired.
If you walk too far
you might never
get back.

3

Don't put problems
in boxes you think
you can seal.
They'll leak out
and colonize.

4

Problems are lumpy.
Don't sweep them
under the carpet.
The carpets will
make hills.

5

Hills are to climb
or to tumble down.
Make sure there's
someone around
to pick you up.

Unhinged

I ask you to oil
the hinges on the screen door
can't you hear them
squeak
      the sound of fingernails
scratching old paint
listen to it flake off

the one that was always
the top one
fastening the door to its frame
is gone
      and the door without it
to hang on
falls halfway out of the cupboard
unhinged
the rusted screw gone

Once I sat in a Bedouin's tent
sipping sage tea
watched from a small boat on the Ganges
how the sun came up
saw my face in a pond
with a hundred-year-old carp

What lasts
is only there in the mind
that holds on to it

my shadow's unhinged
the moment I reach out
to touch it

Gaps

My mind crawls over the words I read
falls into the gaps between them
and climbs out again losing
the meaning in every space it comes out of.

Losing the sense of who I was
not knowing who I've become.

My ears are full of everyone speaking
their words tumble out and leave me
alone with myself whoever that is.

It's too late to figure out who I am
and what does that matter now.
What does anything matter
when I can't keep up with the others

and don't know where I'm headed anyway.

Bird Sanctuary next to a Military Cemetery

In my eightieth year I see for the first time
over my fears about the next war
a sudden streak of metallic flame
skimming the trees
or wilder between the wing beats
a bolt of beaked lightning
                         Kingfisher
ecstatic missile fired from a grave.

I stare at the emptiness it leaves.
A lost iridescence bursts from the footlights
at the Ballet Russe — Riabouchinska's jeté
in *Le Coq d'Or* — the way she springs
out of the wounded world.

                         Green mercy
hovers next to the dead. Who planted
these almonds, this affable meadow?
A blackbird sings a duet in its own two voices
a sunbird tipples from a glass mouth
bulbuls nibble peanuts and persimmons.

In the pond an old crow flutters its wings
like tutus in a rain shower.
Sky turns into water
where a woman sees herself
for the first time
                    rippled with plumage.

Pushing

You keep me
young I tell you
the way I do always
though it's not at all true

so I go on squirting
and spraying
putting my strawberry
lipstick on

leaving myself
little notes
all over the place
so I won't forget

if I find them
I'll still know
what I have to
remember.

So I go on pushing
my body up the hill
the way I keep
scrubbing pots

with steel wool after
the pad is worn out.
I'm not ready
to throw it away.

Late Love Poem

I need your hands
to hold and shape me
smooth my rough edges
into something new.

I'd like to be soft bread
fresh from the oven
fragrant and warm
about to be nibbled.

If we could wrap
our old selves
around each other
we could bake

more than a loaf
of bread we could
sing blessings
as we break it sing

love sing life
make the end wait.
Oh hold me now
because it's late.

Old Poets

All the old poets are writing
about their young loves
on the Oriental rugs of their
parents' living rooms
with the parents upstairs

or in their borrowed cars
as if something sticky
or forbidden still ignites them
though they'd feel silly spreading
a blanket under the stars.

Perhaps because it all seems
desperate even the lure
that isn't usually there
but has to be pumped up
now and then to make sure

you're still alive and capable
of writing about arousal.
What other subject means
as much to anyone
who no longer does it.

Amazement

Nothing makes any sense where
I live and nothing made much sense
where I came from, the parts
didn't work.

What I learned best
was to pretend. That made me feel
different from everyone else.
They skipped me in school

from the third grade to fifth
which was even more different
so it was impossible for me
to fit. Fitting is what matters

like sharing your bed
with the right one. Try telling
the non-fitters. Everyone else
is already in the corrective

facility, everyone else is already
being programmed. So what
can you do? It's like flunking
the course in self-improvement.

You'll have to stay with the dummies
in the used-car lot that's non-corrective.
Rust your heart out. There's nowhere
to go. Old maps have been folded

so long they split at the crease.
If everyone's lost on the roads,
you might as well fly. You might even
enjoy what's left of your life

in a state of amazement. I meant
to say "acceptance." But it came out
like this. My slips are the best
part. The part that's true.

Escape

Words wanting to be wise
slip out and change,
they take another shape
outside my mouth.
Thoughts I used to save
escape.
        To where? I can't
recite the things
I used to know.

Canaries flutter
in the mine shafts
until the end, when
there's no place else to go.

Annapolis

Summits and rifts we seem
to be talking about mountains
maybe we are — how to get over
or through them without losing
our way. The disputes deepen
conflicts continue and promises
to meet again anywhere anytime
the easiest way to get nowhere.

Politicians have done their best
to dance around the issue.
Long-term uncertainties and risks.
Cross-country travel or hostile
borders, hazardous detours
for roads under repair. But what
are we arguing about? Where
do we think we are headed?

December 2007

Streets

The small rooms on the top floors
are lookouts, captains' cabins
on a ship crossing the blue sky
over Jerusalem. We follow
our footsteps up Rashba.
Down Dunash ben Labrat.
We remember his graceful doe
her only son in her arms.

I know just a few of the famous
our streets are named after.
It would take a lifetime to learn them,
and I haven't got time. Pinsker,
Agron. It's good they threw in
Chopin and King George.
And they made a place for Disraeli.
Though my tongue's twisted by Abarbanel.

It's too warm for December,
but that's what I like. Sun on my hair
and the heat trickling all over
my face. I lift my head high
to let it run down my skin.
It stops where my jacket zips
under my chin. I'm glad I won't be a name
on a street. I'm glad I'm not dead.

The ceiling was vaulted

and made me look up
as soon as I walked through the door.

Too lofty for anyone's ambition
whatever it was. Beyond the reach of how high
I could climb. It seemed to be backing away
from where I was standing.
It made me dizzy.

I look up too much. I used to lie on the grass
while the sky filtered through everything
even my arms when I held them out in the air
as if I were praying. When I stared at my hands
I saw the slippery bones in my fingers.

If I look at anything too long I can see
right through it. Even the small
shreds of memory floating past.
Not more than shreds.
I lost all the substance long ago.

I need a thick blanket around me.
I need a heavy canvas over my head
to keep out whatever blows fiercely
through my head. I need a new language
that I can make love in again.

Hiding

Pushed into the back of the closet
to get it out of the way
and then forgotten
until I found it crouched over itself
and curled up like a stray animal
hiding itself from the light.

The way I used to think
if I hid myself under my blankets
where I could see no one
no one could see me.

And I was changing
able to feel the change as it
happened. Running
my fingers over my face.

Unrecognized. No one
would know who I was
when I came out of the bed
where I'd been hiding

no one would know
I was wearing another face.

Seder, 2008/5768

Air woolly with sleep and all of us
dozing around the table trying
to stay awake. After the seder
and after the little wet boats
of chopped fish, crumbs and eggs,
and soup with the lighter-than-air
dumplings, and don't forget
to hide the *afikoman*
so a diligent child can pull
all the books off the shelves
to find it, which someone not only
does but gets paid for.
                                    After
the songs we like to remember
and after the little ones leave the table
to play or sleep whatever they do
when they need to get out of what
grown-ups are doing
someone remembers to
open the door for Elijah
who still hasn't come.
                                    After
we put on our coats and say goodbye
we drive home sad/glad that it's over
till the next year, the next year,
the next when we'll always gather
to remember escaping
over and over and over again.

Directions

What would you say what would you
have to say that is if someone asked you
to say something about what

does it depend on what you would say
or what you would want to say if
you could discover the words or knew
where they came from or where they were
hiding? There you go blaming the words
for not coming out of their hideouts
when the truth is you couldn't discover them
even right under your nose.
                                        Even
two- or three-letter words like
to or *put*
              the most simple directions
since you have to start with directions
how else would you know where
you're going? Or where to begin?

So let's start with your nose
that you almost fell on today
when you fell on your knees
and skinned them the way you used to
when you were a child and fell down often
trying to find what you can't remember.

So much you can't remember now
you might as well stop trying

you'll never live long enough
to get it all back even the things
you still remember that matter the most.

Still Ready

Dawn turns the day
fuzzy as peaches
I can still taste your kiss
from last night.

I can still stay
inside my last dream
gathering blackberries
in a pail
licking the juice
on my fingers

making me feel I was
in our first life
ready to be picked
waiting to be tasted
to take my first bite.

Connected

as if plugged in
not joined
but something deeper
not what I'd hear
on the phone coming from
somewhere outside me
but within
        a whisper
on the tip of your tongue
wordless
as if you had entered me
for the first time
knowing the way

Wanting

to be desired
or even to desire

and needing your arms
around me
         not like a father
soothing a child not like
I need to hang on

but feeling
my wanting still
         and yours
holding each other

where can we go
if not together
how else can we
be so comfortable

so sure
      that we're
           loved

Eighty-five

It's only a number
I've come to, not aging, just
getting riper. I wonder how long
I'll stay ripe without rotting.
I'm already softer than I
used to be, squishy in places
if you press too hard. Mostly
my brain, which doesn't take
too much pressure to weaken.

Not really weaken, but lose
its resistance is what I'm
starting to feel, as if living
had begun to bruise it. It's
easy to find the vulnerable
places in something wobbly
as the mind, which can't
hang on to anything as long
as it needs it or ought to.

Lately I think that most of
what comes out of my mouth
is twaddle. I'm down
in the dumps or up in a tree
with frail branches that look like
they're starting to break
when I bend them. It will be
a quick fall to the bottom
where the ground is.

Finding Our Way

What are we doing
losing ourselves
in newsprint each day
as if words were a rippling
stream we could float in.
Why aren't we afraid
of drowning
          we're afraid
of so much that's less
dangerous. Whispering
strangers. Stepping off
a cliff in the dark.

We can paddle out of
a problem or find
our own way
to the shore.
          There's always
a shore always a magic lamp
for believers who need
to believe.

Peace Rose

The sun is just coming up
colors bloom out of the dark
like roses opening
in the warm air
the petals slowly tip
backward to let the light in.

No fury of fire no spin
of passion it softly opens
petal by petal to the heart
of its quiet like a long
breath slowly exhaled.

Notes

page 17 *Succot* (also *Sukkoth*): The Jewish autumn festival of thanksgiving that celebrates the first harvest.

page 53 *hupa* (also *huppah*): A wedding canopy under which the bride and groom stand.

page 61 *We will become godlike:* From C.D. Wright, *Deepstep Come Shining*, 1998.

About the Author

Shirley Kaufman was born in Seattle, lived in San Francisco, and immigrated to Jerusalem in 1973 when she married H.M. (Bill) Daleski, professor emeritus, The Hebrew University. Eight volumes of her poetry have been published in the United States, most recently *Roots in the Air: New and Selected Poems* (1996) and *Threshold* (2003), both from Copper Canyon Press. This is her ninth collection.

Kaufman won the United States Award of the International Poetry Forum, for her first book of poems, in 1969. Among her many awards since then are two grants from the National Endowment for the Arts, a Rockefeller Foundation residency at Bellagio, the Pushcart Prize, the Shelley Memorial Award for lifetime achievement from the Poetry Society of America, and the Israel President's Prize for literature by a writer in English, in 2007. A volume of her selected poems was published in Hebrew by Bialik Press in 1995, translated by Aharon Shabtai, and a bilingual volume of her poems, translated into French by Claude Vigée, was published by Cheyne éditeur in 2003.

The Chinese character for poetry is made up of two parts: "word" and "temple." It also serves as pressmark for Copper Canyon Press.

Since 1972, Copper Canyon Press has fostered the work of emerging, established, and world-renowned poets for an expanding audience. The Press thrives with the generous patronage of readers, writers, booksellers, librarians, teachers, students, and funders—everyone who shares the belief that poetry is vital to language and living.

Major funding has been provided by:

Amazon.com

Anonymous

Beroz Ferrell & The Point, LLC

Cynthia Hartwig and Tom Booster

Golden Lasso, LLC

Lannan Foundation

National Endowment for the Arts

Cynthia Lovelace Sears and Frank Buxton

Washington State Arts Commission

For information and catalogs:

COPPER CANYON PRESS
Post Office Box 271
Port Townsend, Washington 98368
360-385-4925
www.coppercanyonpress.org

—

The interior is set in Miller, a "Scotch Roman" designed by Matthew
Carter in 1997. The display type is Bell, the digital version of type cut
in 1788 by Richard Austin for publisher John Bell. Book design by
Valerie Brewster, Scribe Typography. Printed at BookMobile.